DEVOTIONAL BIBLE SERIES VOLUME 2

A BACKSLIDING HEART

Things We Never Got Over

CHARLES MORRIS

Copyright © 2023 Charles W Morris

All rights reserved. No part of this book may be used or reproduced by any means, graphic, electronic, or mechanical, including photocopying, recording, taping, or by any information storage retrieval system without the written permission of the publisher except in the case of brief quotations embodied in critical articles and reviews.

Scriptures are taken from the English Standard Version of the Bible
Books may be ordered through booksellers or by contacting:
RSIP
Raising the Standard International Publishing LLC
https://www.rsipublishing.com

RSIP-Charles Morris
https://www.rsiministry.com
Navarre, Florida

ISBN: 9781960641311
Printed in the United States of America
Edition Date: November 2023

TABLE OF CONTENTS

1	What Is Backsliding?	1
2	Is Backsliding Biblical?	7
3	How Does God Feel About A Backslidden Heart?	14
4	The Consequences Of A Backslidden Heart	17
5	Pride Leads Us To A Backslidden Heart	32
6	A Backsliding Heart Will Continue In That Direction And Increase In Unrighteous Behavior	35
7	The Father Exhorts, "Return To Me"	38
8	The Consequences Of Backsliding	40
9	God Will Punishment Those Who Tempt Others To Backslide	43
10	How Can We Help Someone Who Is Backsliding?	47
11	There Is Hope For The Backslider	51
12	Prayers Of Confession In Turning Away From The Sin Of Backsliding	53
13	Promises From The Father That He Will Pardon The Backslider	58
14	The Father Will Heal The Heart Of The Backslider	60

15	There Is A Blessing For Those Who Keep Themselves From A Heart Of Backsliding	62
	More Books By Charles Morris	67
	About The Author	69

Chapter 1
WHAT IS BACKSLIDING?

We used to hear years ago about people who were backslidden and out of fellowship with God and the body of Christ. We don't hear much about it anymore. Why is that? Have we grown so accustomed to sin within the church that it is no longer an issue? Have we misused the phrase "you are just judging" so much that we have assumed that anything goes and we are not our brother's keeper? Are there things we never got over before getting saved that seem to have a stronghold in our lives?

We need to revisit the sin of "backsliding" and how it affects us individually and corporately as the body of Christ.

The word "backslide" can have many connotations based on who we speak with. We may even know people we consider backsliders. However, what does backslide even mean from a Biblical definition? If we write about this topic, we must ensure we are discussing the same thing. Though people have different ideas of what backslide means, the definition that best fits is one sliding back from their closeness to Christ or walking away from their first love. For some reason, this person is growing cold in their relationship and fellowship with Jesus (and sometimes engaging in behavior that portrays their life before Christ).

Although the teaching of a backslidden heart is in the New Testament, the term backslide appears only in the Old Testament, referring most often to the people of Israel. They fit into the "backslider" category because they were God's people. None of the other pagan nations were ever called backsliders. The shadow of God's plan is found in the Old Testament in the Law, while the substance is found in the New Testament in our Lord Jesus Christ. We know if we, as believers, repent and return to the Lord, He is faithful to forgive us and cleanse us from all unrighteousness. However, in most of this study, I will use Old Testament Scriptures to show that our returning to the Lord from a backslidden condition has always been on the Father's heart. The call of the Father for us to return echoes throughout the Scriptures.

> *1 John 1:9 (ESV) If we confess our sins, he is faithful and just to forgive us our sins and to cleanse us from all unrighteousness.*

It is a reasonable question to ask if Christians can truly backslide. The answer is simple. Not only can Christians backslide, but they are also the only ones who can. Remember, a critical aspect of being a backslider is being a faithful Christian first. If a person was never in a relationship with Jesus Christ, they can't backslide. You can't walk away from something you never possessed.

Therefore, backsliding simply means "turning one's back on God." Ironically, God's people backslide mostly after times of great blessing and prosperity. Often, when God poured out incredible mercies in Israel, the people soon turned away from Him. Let's look at some of the critical aspects of backsliding.

1. Backsliding Is Turning Away From God

Backsliding is a willful choice to turn away from walking with God. The backsliding of the heart can happen even if outward religious activity, such as church attendance, increases. Just because we "love" the things of God does not mean we love God. Doing Christian discipline mandates such as praying, reading your Bible, and attending church does not mean that we are walking in fellowship with God.

> *1 Kings 11:9 (ESV) And the LORD was angry with Solomon, because his heart had turned away from the LORD, the God of Israel, who had appeared to him twice*

2. Backsliding Is Leaving Or Forsaking Your First Love

Forsaking fellowship with the Father is not "losing our first love" but a willful walking away from the first love. I have found that this is usually replaced by whatever is necessary at the moment. The "first love" could be replaced with work, a spouse, children, money, apathy, church, or love for the world.

> Revelation 2:4 (ESV) But I have this against you, that you have abandoned the love you had at first.

3. Backsliding Is Departing From The Simplicity Of The Gospel

People with backslidden hearts move in one or two ways. They may walk away from God, the church, and any religious activities to do what is right in their own eyes. The second way people who are backslidden react will be to establish a set of rules and laws for themselves and others. People in sin and who are dull of hearing seldom judge themselves based on God's Word and His character. Instead of evaluating their condition of being out of fellowship with the Father, they judge themselves on their ability to maintain their established religious rules and boundaries.

The apostle Paul tells the Corinth believers in 2 Corinthians 11:3-4 that they could be led astray from a sincere and pure devotion to Christ. Then, the apostle gives some of the ways we can backslide.

> 2 Corinthians 11:3-4 (ESV) But I am afraid that as the serpent deceived Eve by his cunning,

your thoughts will be led astray from a sincere and pure devotion to Christ. 4 For if someone comes and proclaims another Jesus than the one we proclaimed, or if you receive a different spirit from the one you received, or if you accept a different gospel from the one you accepted, you put up with it readily enough.

In Galatians 3:1-3 the apostle Paul warns the believers not to move from walking in the Spirit to walking in the flesh. This spiritual shift would be exchanging fellowship with Christ for religious activity, which is becoming like the Pharisees.

Galatians 3:1-3 (ESV) O foolish Galatians! Who has bewitched you? It was before your eyes that Jesus Christ was publicly portrayed as crucified. 2 Let me ask you only this: Did you receive the Spirit by works of the law or by hearing with faith? 3 Are you so foolish? Having begun by the Spirit, are you now being perfected by the flesh?

The three aspects of Christian life are to start well, run well, and finish well. Paul scolded the Galatians, who started well and ran well but got sidetracked and faced the risk of ending badly.

Galatians 5:4-7 (ESV) You are severed from Christ, you who would be justified by the law; you have fallen away from grace. 5 For through the Spirit, by faith, we ourselves eagerly wait for the hope of righteousness. 6 For in Christ Jesus neither circumcision nor uncircumcision counts for anything, but only faith working through love. 7 You were running well. Who hindered you from obeying the truth?

Chapter 2
IS BACKSLIDING BIBLICAL?

Any doctrine we believe to be accurate, and Biblical needs to have an Old Testament shadow and a New Testament substance. A preacher once said, "The Bible never says anything about backsliding." That man doesn't know his Bible! The Scriptures speak much about backsliding because it is a grave matter with severe consequences!

Let's see what the Old Testament says. The term "backslider" is used sixteen times in the Old Testament. Twelve of the sixteen uses of the word backslider are used in the book of Jeremiah. There are different Hebrew words based on their usage.

1. Backslider: Translated As "Turned Away."

In Proverbs 14:14 and Jeremiah 8:5, "Backslider" means the "turning of the foot." To turn around or change directions.

> *Proverbs 14:14 (ESV) The backslider in heart will be filled with the fruit of his ways, and a good man will be filled with the fruit of his ways.*

Jeremiah 8:5 (ESV) Why then has this people turned away in perpetual backsliding? They hold fast to deceit; they refuse to return.

2. Backsliding: Translated As "Apostasy, Apostasies, Faithless One, and Faithless."

What is the difference between backsliding and apostasy? Backsliding is a sliding away from fellowship with God the Father, Son, and Holy Spirit. Although backsliding is not sudden in onset, it may escalate rapidly once it starts. Backsliding is different from falling away from the faith or apostasy. Apostasy is the extreme end of backsliding. Apostasy or falling away is the act or state of rejecting the Christian Faith and belief in the Lord Jesus Christ.

In Jeremiah 2:19, 3:6, 3:8, 3:11-12, 3:14, 3:22, 5:6, 8:5, 14:17, Hosea 11:7, and Hosea 14:4, the Hebrew words that make up the term "backsliding" means "Press to the tent." It refers to turning away from a place of dwelling. Therefore, backsliding means turning away or committing apostasy.

APOSTASY

In Jeremiah 2:19, backsliding is translated as "apostasy," meaning to desert or walk away from the faith, a turning away from your dwelling place.

Jeremiah 2:19 (ESV) Your evil will chastise you, and your apostasy will reprove you. Know and see that it is evil and bitter for you to forsake the LORD your God; the fear of me is not in you, declares the Lord GOD of hosts.

Hosea 14:4 (ESV) I will heal their apostasy; I will love them freely, for my anger has turned from them.

APOSTASIES

In Jeremiah 5:6, backsliding is translated as "apostasies," which also means to desert or walk away from the faith, a turning away from your dwelling place.

Jeremiah 5:6 (ESV) Therefore a lion from the forest shall strike them down; a wolf from the desert shall devastate them. A leopard is watching their cities; everyone who goes out of them shall be torn in pieces, because their transgressions are many, their apostasies are great.

BACKSLIDING

In Jeremiah 8:5 and 14:7, backsliding is the word "backsliding," which also means to desert or walk away from the faith, a turning away from a dwelling place.

Jeremiah 8:5 (ESV) Why then has this people turned away in perpetual backsliding? They hold fast to deceit; they refuse to return.

Jeremiah 14:7 (ESV) "Though our iniquities testify against us, act, O LORD, for your name's sake; for our backslidings are many; we have sinned against you.

FAITHLESS ONE

In Jeremiah 3:6 and 3:8, backsliding is translated as "faithless one," which also means to desert or walk away from the faith, which are those who turn away from a place of dwelling.

Jeremiah 3:6 (ESV) The LORD said to me in the days of King Josiah: "Have you seen what she did, that faithless one, Israel, how she went up on every high hill and under every green tree, and there played the whore?

Jeremiah 3:8 (ESV) She saw that for all the adulteries of that faithless one, Israel, I had sent her away with a decree of divorce. Yet her treacherous sister Judah did not fear, but she too went and played the whore.

FAITHLESS

In Jeremiah 3:11-12, 14, and 22, backsliding is translated as "faithless," which also means to desert or walk away from the faith, which are those who turn away from a place of dwelling.

A BACKSLIDING HEART

Jeremiah 3:11 (ESV) And the LORD said to me, "Faithless Israel has shown herself more righteous than treacherous Judah.

Jeremiah 3:12 (ESV) Go, and proclaim these words toward the north, and say, "'Return, faithless Israel, declares the LORD. I will not look on you in anger, for I am merciful, declares the LORD; I will not be angry forever.

Jeremiah 3:14 (ESV) Return, O faithless children, declares the LORD; for I am your master; I will take you, one from a city and two from a family, and I will bring you to Zion.

Jeremiah 3:22 (ESV) "Return, O faithless sons; I will heal your faithlessness." "Behold, we come to you, for you are the LORD our God.

TURNING AWAY

Hosea 11:7 (ESV) My people are bent on turning away from me, and though they call out to the Most High, he shall not raise them up at all.

3. **Backsliding: Translated As Faithless.**

In Jeremiah 31:22 and 49:4, "Backsliding" means "apostate, heathen, or heathenish." It is a harder word because it means to return to a previous place or dwelling. For us, it would mean to return to the place before we were saved.

Jeremiah 31:22 (ESV) How long will you waver, O faithless daughter? For the LORD has created a new thing on the earth: a woman encircles a man."

Jeremiah 49:4 (ESV) Why do you boast of your valleys, O faithless daughter, who trusted in her treasures, saying, 'Who will come against me?'

2 Peter 2:20-22 (ESV) For if, after they have escaped the defilements of the world through the knowledge of our Lord and Savior Jesus Christ, they are again entangled in them and overcome, the last state has become worse for them than the first. 21 For it would have been better for them never to have known the way of righteousness than after knowing it to turn back from the holy commandment delivered to them. 22 What the true proverb says has happened to them: "The dog returns to its own vomit, and the sow, after washing herself, returns to wallow in the mire."

4. Backsliding: Translated As Stubborn.

In Hosea 4:16, "Backsliding" means "stubborn, slide back, rebellious, revolt, and withdrew." This is where we get the word "stiff-necked." The term is used twice in Hosea 4:16.

A BACKSLIDING HEART

Hosea 4:16 (ESV) Like a stubborn heifer, Israel is stubborn; can the LORD now feed them like a lamb in a broad pasture?

Chapter 3
HOW DOES GOD FEEL ABOUT A BACKSLIDDEN HEART?

When we make decisions about sin, we may have the tendency to make decisions based on what others feel about the sin. The key is to look in the Word and see how God views our sins. We need our hearts to feel the same about sin as the Father thinks about it.

1. **God Is Displeased With A Backslidden Heart**

What does God say about backsliding? Even though God loves us, He absolutely hates our backsliding. We must establish in our hearts that our heavenly Father is greatly displeased with backsliding.

> *Psalms 78:57-59 (ESV) but turned away and acted treacherously like their fathers; they twisted like a deceitful bow. 58 For they provoked him to anger with their high places; they moved him to jealousy with their idols. 59 When God heard, he was full of wrath, and he utterly rejected Israel.*

A BACKSLIDING HEART

Therefore, He strongly entreats every Christian to be wary of and watch against backsliding and to support and encourage other Christians in the faith.

Hebrews 3:12-13 (ESV) Take care, brothers, lest there be in any of you an evil, unbelieving heart, leading you to fall away from the living God. 13 But exhort one another every day, as long as it is called "today," that none of you may be hardened by the deceitfulness of sin.

There are consequences for the backsliding Christian. In God's rebuke of the nation of Israel, he equates backsliding with worshipping idols, which is a severe offense.

Proverbs 14:14 (ESV) The backslider in heart will be filled with the fruit of his ways, and a good man will be filled with the fruit of his ways.

2. God Warns Against A Backslidden Heart

God views backsliding as folly and warns that we shall fall away if we remain in it. Backsliding begins in the heart long before the outward evidence is manifested.

Psalms 85:8 (ESV) Let me hear what God the LORD will speak, for he will speak peace to his

> *people, to his saints; but let them not turn back to folly.*
>
> *1 Corinthians 10:12 (ESV) Therefore let anyone who thinks that he stands take heed lest he fall.*

In studying the Apostle Paul's letter to the Galatians, I encountered his words in Galatians 5:4. He says, "You who are trying to be justified by the law have been alienated from Christ; you have fallen away from grace."

What does it mean to fall away from grace? The verse clearly implies that those who once embraced grace and faith and then, through pride and a backslidden heart, started looking to the law for their justification separated themselves from Christ. They are turning away or departing from God's provision of grace in the cross of Christ.

> *Galatians 5:4-7 (ESV) You are severed from Christ, you who would be justified by the law; you have fallen away from grace. 5 For through the Spirit, by faith, we ourselves eagerly wait for the hope of righteousness. 6 For in Christ Jesus neither circumcision nor uncircumcision counts for anything, but only faith working through love. 7 You were running well. Who hindered you from obeying the truth?*

CHAPTER 4
THE CONSEQUENCES OF A BACKSLIDDEN HEART

We always talk about the need we have to walk with the Lord. But there is something more important than that. It is maintaining a position of fellowship where the Lord walks with us. When our hearts are backslidden, we forfeit fellowship and the joy of the daily presence of the Lord. When you are backslidden, you are dangerous to be around.

We all know the story of Jonah and how he tried to run from God. Backslidden Jonah was a marked man who knew God would not let him escape his rebellion. Jonah became dangerous to anyone around him when he stepped onto the boat at Joppa. Why? God was after Jonah to fulfill what God wanted him to do!

When God has an issue with a backslider, it affects everyone around him. When the backslider's storm finally comes, it hits everybody. That includes family, children, coworkers, friends, and even strangers. The storm aimed at Jonah put everyone on that ship in danger, along with the dozens of other vessels on that part of the sea. Hundreds, perhaps thousands, of lives were exposed to the great risk.

For years, I've heard backslidden Christians say, "My life is my life and my problem only. I'm not hurting anyone but myself." No! Scripture proves that it's not just your problem. No man is an island unto himself. It's the problem of everyone who lives with you, walks with you, knows you. God warns us to separate ourselves from those walking in sin.

> *Psalms 1:1-3 (ESV) Blessed is the man who walks not in the counsel of the wicked, nor stands in the way of sinners, nor sits in the seat of scoffers; 2 but his delight is in the law of the LORD, and on his law he meditates day and night. 3 He is like a tree planted by streams of water that yields its fruit in its season, and its leaf does not wither. In all that he does, he prospers.*

However, things are not so well with the backslider. God pursues the backslider. And those who are hanging around them are in a dangerous position!

> *Psalms 1:4-6 (ESV) The wicked are not so, but are like chaff that the wind drives away. 5 Therefore the wicked will not stand in the judgment, nor sinners in the congregation of the righteous; 6 for the LORD knows the way of the righteous, but the way of the wicked will perish.*

A BACKSLIDING HEART

Beloved, nobody lives and dies only to himself! David sinned by numbering the Israelites. King David became a dangerous man to be around. The judgment that God sent on David fell on Israel as well. Talk about a deadly storm: 70,000 men lost their lives! King David cried out to God.

> *2 Samuel 24:17 (ESV) Then David spoke to the LORD when he saw the angel who was striking the people, and said, "Behold, I have sinned, and I have done wickedly. But these sheep, what have they done? Please let your hand be against me and against my father's house."*

What about modern-day backslidden believers? At one time, these believers were a bold testimony for our Lord Jesus Christ. on the job. They may have kept their Bibles on their desks and were always eager and ready to share their faith in Jesus. But their coworkers knew something had changed and genuinely different about their resident Christian. The spiritually lost and ungodly coworkers realize there has been a change in the one who once proclaimed salvation and changed life in no one but Jesus.

They know their Christian colleague is backslidden! They may not use that word. Most would call the backslidden Christian a hypocrite. They can't explain what has happened in spiritual terms, but they do know something is different, and he is not the Christian man he once was.

Their once-zealous Christian coworker who preached eternal life or eternal damnation has become like them. They may have mocked him at one time, but secretly, they respected him and knew he was someone they could go to for advice if they were in trouble.

This backslidden Christian has taken away what little spark of faith and hope they might have had. Now, the coworkers are convinced that serving God for any amount of time and consistency is impossible. When we backslide from the Lord or walk away from our first love, we are in danger of forfeiting many things. Let's let the Word speak for itself.

1. In Backsliding, We Forfeit God's Protection

> *Numbers 14:43 (ESV) For there the Amalekites and the Canaanites are facing you, and you shall fall by the sword. Because you have turned back from following the LORD, the LORD will not be with you."*

We find many examples in the Bible where God's people failed because God was no longer with them. They still made a futile attempt in the flesh and in their strength and intellect to accomplish what they had rejected by faith, ending in defeat. Those who backslid and rebelled against God's plan ended up in

A BACKSLIDING HEART

the wilderness. The wilderness was literal with Israel but can be financial, relational, or other means God deems as the consequences of our rebellion. Israel often acted like God was not enough when they had Him close. Then, when God pulled back His protection and presence because of their backslidden hearts, they thought they could live fine without Him.

2. In Backsliding, We Forfeit Freedom

Psalms 125:4-5 (ESV) Do good, O LORD, to those who are good, and to those who are upright in their hearts! 5 But those who turn aside to their crooked ways the LORD will lead away with evildoers! Peace be upon Israel!

The Apostle Paul tells us to stand fast in the liberty we have in faith and grace and not to be in bondage to the Law again. Rebellion and a backslidden heart drive us to the religion of man over the fellowship with our Lord.

Galatians 5:1 (ESV) For freedom Christ has set us free; stand firm therefore, and do not submit again to a yoke of slavery.

3. In Backsliding, We Forfeit Fellowship

Isaiah 59:1-2 (ESV) Behold, the LORD's hand is not shortened, that it cannot save, or his ear dull, that it cannot hear; 2 but your iniquities have made a separation between you and your

God, and your sins have hidden his face from you so that he does not hear.

Our fellowship as believers must be in the faith and walking in the Spirit. If we walk in the Spirit, we will not fulfill the deeds of the flesh.

1 John 1:3 (ESV) that which we have seen and heard we proclaim also to you, so that you too may have fellowship with us; and indeed our fellowship is with the Father and with his Son Jesus Christ.

The Scriptures teach us to separate ourselves from unruly Christians. Paul tells us to separate ourselves from Christian brothers who are unruly or disorderly in Word and deed. This could be separating from an individual or a corporate body of believers. If we walk in sin, we forfeit fellowship.

Romans 16:17-18 (ESV) I appeal to you, brothers, to watch out for those who cause divisions and create obstacles contrary to the doctrine that you have been taught; avoid them. 18 For such persons do not serve our Lord Christ, but their own appetites, and by smooth talk and flattery they deceive the hearts of the naive.

2 Thessalonians 3:6 (ESV) Now we command you, brothers, in the name of our Lord Jesus Christ, that you keep away from any brother who is walking in idleness and not in accord with the tradition that you received from us.

2 Thessalonians 3:14-15 (ESV) If anyone does not obey what we say in this letter, take note of that person, and have nothing to do with him, that he may be ashamed. 15 Do not regard him as an enemy, but warn him as a brother.

Titus 3:10-11 (ESV) As for a person who stirs up division, after warning him once and then twice, have nothing more to do with him, 11 knowing that such a person is warped and sinful; he is self-condemned.

1 Corinthians 5:11-13 (ESV) But now I am writing to you not to associate with anyone who bears the name of brother if he is guilty of sexual immorality or greed, or is an idolater, reviler, drunkard, or swindler—not even to eat with such a one. 12 For what have I to do with judging outsiders? Is it not those inside the church whom you are to judge? 13 God judges those outside. "Purge the evil person from among you."

4. In Backsliding, We Forfeit Hope

Isaiah 59:11-13 (ESV) We all growl like bears; we moan and moan like doves; we hope for justice, but there is none; for salvation, but it is far from us. 12 For our transgressions are multiplied before you, and our sins testify

> against us; for our transgressions are with us, and we know our iniquities: 13 transgressing, and denying the LORD, and turning back from following our God, speaking oppression and revolt, conceiving and uttering from the heart lying words.

The most significant danger of backsliding is committing apostasy. We continue in sin until we return to our old life and walk away from the faith. At that point, we forfeit hope.

> 2 Peter 2:20-22 (ESV) For if, after they have escaped the defilements of the world through the knowledge of our Lord and Savior Jesus Christ, they are again entangled in them and overcome, the last state has become worse for them than the first. 21 For it would have been better for them never to have known the way of righteousness than after knowing it to turn back from the holy commandment delivered to them. 22 What the true proverb says has happened to them: "The dog returns to its own vomit, and the sow, after washing herself, returns to wallow in the mire."

5. In Backsliding, We Forfeit All Morals

> Jeremiah 5:6-7 (ESV) Therefore a lion from the forest shall strike them down; a wolf from the desert shall devastate them. A leopard is watching their cities; everyone who goes out of them shall be torn in pieces, because their

transgressions are many, their apostasies are great. 7 "How can I pardon you? Your children have forsaken me and have sworn by those who are no gods. When I fed them to the full, they committed adultery and trooped to the houses of whores.

When I was growing up, I was told by my parents not to hang around bad people. Little did they know I was that wrong person and spoiled the morals of many. I say this in my shame and am certainly not proud of it.

1 Corinthians 15:33 (ESV) Do not be deceived: "Bad company ruins good morals."

6. **In Backsliding, We Forfeit Truth And The Desire To Repent**

Jeremiah 8:4-6 (ESV) "You shall say to them, Thus says the LORD: When men fall, do they not rise again? If one turns away, does he not return? 5 Why then has this people turned away in perpetual backsliding? They hold fast to deceit; they refuse to return. 6 I have paid attention and listened, but they have not spoken rightly; no man relents of his evil, saying, 'What have I done?' Everyone turns to his own course, like a horse plunging headlong into battle.

We know from Romans 10:17 that faith comes by hearing and hearing by the Word. But when we sin and walk in rebellion as backsliders, we grow dull of hearing. If we don't hear the truth, we are open to all forms of deception.

> *Hebrews 5:11-13 (ESV) About this we have much to say, and it is hard to explain, since you have become dull of hearing. 12 For though by this time you ought to be teachers, you need someone to teach you again the basic principles of the oracles of God. You need milk, not solid food, 13 for everyone who lives on milk is unskilled in the word of righteousness, since he is a child.*

7. In Backsliding, We Forfeit The Conscience To Be Ashamed

I am shocked at what I see and hear on TV and social media. People have become so calloused, hard-hearted, and lawless that nothing embarrasses them, and they feel no shame. This national lawlessness started within the hearts of each individual as they turned away from any wooing of the Holy Spirit.

> *Jeremiah 8:12 (ESV) Were they ashamed when they committed abomination? No, they were not at all ashamed; they did not know how to blush. Therefore they shall fall among the fallen; when I punish them, they shall be overthrown, says the LORD.*

A BACKSLIDING HEART

> *Matthew 5:19-20 (ESV) Therefore whoever relaxes one of the least of these commandments and teaches others to do the same will be called least in the kingdom of heaven, but whoever does them and teaches them will be called great in the kingdom of heaven. 20 For I tell you, unless your righteousness exceeds that of the scribes and Pharisees, you will never enter the kingdom of heaven.*

As you read 1 Timothy 4:1-2, see that it states that some will depart from the faith. This is backsliding to the point of apostasy and then having the conscience seared.

> *1 Timothy 4:1-2 (ESV) Now the Spirit expressly says that in later times some will depart from the faith by devoting themselves to deceitful spirits and teachings of demons, 2 through the insincerity of liars whose consciences are seared,*

8. In Backsliding, We Forfeit God's Mercy, And We Release His Justice

We talk a lot about the punishment and judgment of sin. But the sin of backsliding carries its own punishment with it. Someone backsliding does what is right in his own heart and creates a situation that leads him further away from the Lord with the danger of causing a hardened and callous heart.

> *Jeremiah 2:19 (ESV) Your evil will chastise you, and your apostasy will reprove you. Know and see that it is evil and bitter for you to forsake the LORD your God; the fear of me is not in you, declares the Lord GOD of hosts.*

> *Jeremiah 15:5-6 (ESV) "Who will have pity on you, O Jerusalem, or who will grieve for you? Who will turn aside to ask about your welfare? 6 You have rejected me, declares the LORD; you keep going backward, so I have stretched out my hand against you and destroyed you— I am weary of relenting.*

When we speak about forfeiting mercy, we see in the Scriptures that some will depart and walk away from God's grace.

> *Galatians 5:4-7 (ESV) You are severed from Christ, you who would be justified by the law; you have fallen away from grace. 5 For through the Spirit, by faith, we ourselves eagerly wait for the hope of righteousness. 6 For in Christ Jesus neither circumcision nor uncircumcision counts for anything, but only faith working through love. 7 You were running well. Who hindered you from obeying the truth?*

9. In Backsliding, We Forfeit Our Place Or Position In The Kingdom

Remember that Judas was a member of our Lord's twelve. He was among the group sent out to heal the sick, cast out demons, and preach the good news. However, something was happening within his heart. He was backsliding and moving away from the Lord. We read in Acts that Judas left his first estate or position. This is apostasy or falling away from the faith.

Acts 1:16-18 (ESV) "Brothers, the Scripture had to be fulfilled, which the Holy Spirit spoke beforehand by the mouth of David concerning Judas, who became a guide to those who arrested Jesus. 17 For he was numbered among us and was allotted his share in this ministry." 18 (Now this man acquired a field with the reward of his wickedness, and falling headlong he burst open in the middle and all his bowels gushed out.

Acts 1:24-25 (ESV) And they prayed and said, "You, Lord, who know the hearts of all, show which one of these two you have chosen 25 to take the place in this ministry and apostleship from which Judas turned aside to go to his own place."

Luke 9:62 (ESV) Jesus said to him, "No one who puts his hand to the plow and looks back is fit for the kingdom of God."

Remember the definition given in chapter two concerning the term "backslidden?" I'll repeat some chapter two info, hoping you understand the connection to Judas.

In Proverbs 14:14 and Jeremiah 8:5, "Backslider" means the "turning of the foot." To turn around or change directions.

In Jeremiah 2:19, backsliding is translated as "apostasy," meaning to desert or walk away from the faith, a turning away from your dwelling place.

In Jeremiah 2:19, 3:6, 3:8, 3:11-12, 3:14, 3:22, 5:6, 8:5, 14:17, Hosea 11:7, and Hosea 14:4, the Hebrew words that make up the term "backsliding" means "Press to the tent." It refers to turning away from a place of dwelling. Therefore, backsliding means turning away or committing apostasy.

In Jeremiah 2:19, backsliding is translated as "apostasy," meaning to desert or walk away from the faith, a turning away from your dwelling place.

Having reread these Biblical definitions, reread Acts 1:24-25 and see how Judas left his house or position with our Lord and the disciples and returned to his own place. This means that he left the faith and returned to his old life.

> *Acts 1:24-25 (ESV) And they prayed and said, "You, Lord, who know the hearts of all, show which one of these two you have chosen 25 to take the place in this ministry and apostleship*

A BACKSLIDING HEART

from which Judas turned aside to go to his own place."

Chapter 5
PRIDE LEADS US TO A BACKSLIDDEN HEART

Someone asked me just the other day, "Pastor, why would anyone in their right mind want to turn away from the Lord once they have tasted the goodness of God?" This is a great question. The number one reason is the neglect of spiritual disciplines. The Word tells us that the church at Ephesus did all the right things except for paying close attention to their hearts. They exceeded in works yet faith in the heart by leaving, abandoning, deserting, their first love.

> *Revelation 2:2-5 (ESV) "'I know your works, your toil and your patient endurance, and how you cannot bear with those who are evil, but have tested those who call themselves apostles and are not, and found them to be false. 3 I know you are enduring patiently and bearing up for my name's sake, and you have not grown weary. 4 But I have this against you, that you have abandoned the love you had at first. 5 Remember therefore from where you have fallen; repent, and do the works you did at first. If not, I will come to you and remove your lampstand from its place, unless you repent.*

A BACKSLIDING HEART

Like the Pharisees, we can become professional Christians. We know how to attend church, tithe, read our Bibles, and pray. However, we fall short of cultivating and maintaining a passionate love relationship of the heart toward our Lord Jesus Christ.

This professional Christian attitude causes us to be prideful and unteachable. This is one of the reasons Pastors have so much frustration and have an average church tenure of less than three years. When people are dull of hearing and unteachable, the voice of the Pastor is just one opinion among the thousands they can get on social media. When we elevate ourselves in our own eyes above others, we set ourselves up for a fall and develop a backslidden heart. By the way, the Scripture in Proverbs 16:18 does not say that "Pride goes before the fall." Pride goes before destruction!

Proverbs 16:18 (ESV) Pride goes before destruction, and a haughty spirit before a fall.

Remember, the main reason behind a Christian backsliding is that they had forsaken their first love somewhere along the way. Something happens that causes their passion for Jesus to go cold. This led them to turn away or fall back into their life before knowing Christ. This can come from neglect, distractions, disappointments, discouragements, hurt, or rebellion, which we are all prone to. Backsliding begins in the heart when we give into self-interest, old habits, and old excuses. It models the third soil in the parable of the four soils in Matthew chapter 13.

Backsliding is a universal experience among the body of Christ. Every one of us, at some time, resists significant change, no matter whether it's for the worse or the better. We desire change as long as it is someone else changing. Our soulish man (thoughts, emotions, and will) has a built-in tendency to stay the same within relatively narrow limits. Even when we change, the familiar or old pattern of life calls us back. We are like water and seek the path of least resistance.

Those who backslide away from the faith are full of pride, unwilling to face the world-ward shame that comes with walking with God.

The shame attached to being a true believer in God's Word lies as a block in their way. It is like the second soil in the parable of the four soils in Matthew, chapter 13. The sun that came out was the plant offended by God's Word. These who backslid may remain proud and arrogant in their religion but shun God's Word and His command to walk in holiness. They return to their former course of life without fear of judgment because their hearts become seared.

CHAPTER 6
A BACKSLIDING HEART WILL CONTINUE IN THAT DIRECTION AND INCREASE IN UNRIGHTEOUS BEHAVIOR

We were taught a great lesson from the life of Pharaoh in the Book of Exodus. It says that he hardened his heart. Then it says that God hardened his heart. It was the Biblical principle that God will continue in us the way of our hearts. If our heart is towards the Father, He will continue that process in us. If our hearts are turned away from God, we will continue in that direction. A backslider will become increasingly insensitive towards sin, and things they once hated become a standard part of everyday life.

> *Jeremiah 8:4-5 (ESV) "You shall say to them, Thus says the LORD: When men fall, do they not rise again? If one turns away, does he not return? 5 Why then has this people turned away in perpetual backsliding? They hold fast to deceit; they refuse to return.*
>
> *Jeremiah 14:7 (ESV) "Though our iniquities testify against us, act, O LORD, for your*

name's sake; for our backslidings are many; we have sinned against you.

Lot did not wake up one day and decided to move to Sodom. Lot pitched his tent in that direction each day for a long time. In other words, Lot was bent in that direction. A person who walks in righteousness is inclined towards the Lord and His ways. A person with a prideful, unrighteous heart is bent towards a backslidden heart and will fall into it.

The point is that Lot never planned to go to Sodom; he planned to settle the plain. But he pitched his tent in the direction of Sodom, and in time, the pull to Sodom was more than his heart could resist. The wicked of heart will fall into mischief.

Genesis 13:10-11 (ESV) And Lot lifted up his eyes and saw that the Jordan Valley was well watered everywhere like the garden of the LORD, like the land of Egypt, in the direction of Zoar. (This was before the LORD destroyed Sodom and Gomorrah.) 11 So Lot chose for himself all the Jordan Valley, and Lot journeyed east. Thus they separated from each other.

Genesis 13:12 (ESV) Abram settled in the land of Canaan, while Lot settled among the cities of the valley and moved his tent as far as Sodom.

A BACKSLIDING HEART

Proverbs 24:16 (ESV) for the righteous falls seven times and rises again, but the wicked stumble in times of calamity.

Hosea 11:7 (ESV) My people are bent on turning away from me, and though they call out to the Most High, he shall not raise them up at all.

Chapter 7
THE FATHER EXHORTS, "RETURN TO ME"

The Father is calling for us to turn away from a backsliding heart and return our hearts to him. It is never in our Father's heart for us to remain in sin, nor does the Father tolerate or condone sin. When our hearts are in a backslidden condition, the Father exhorts us to repent and return to Him. Softly and tenderly, our Lord is calling, "Come home, Come home."

I know 2 Chronicles 7:14 deals with Israel and the temple. However, it is still a principle that the Father would honor if a nation would turn to Him. But how about an individual or a group of Christians meeting together, calling for the Lord to heal their hearts, homes, and communities? Yes, I believe the Father would honor such a cry of repentance.

> *2 Chronicles 7:14 (ESV) if my people who are called by my name humble themselves, and pray and seek my face and turn from their wicked ways, then I will hear from heaven and will forgive their sin and heal their land.*
>
> *2 Chronicles 30:6-9 (ESV) So couriers went throughout all Israel and Judah with letters*

A BACKSLIDING HEART

from the king and his princes, as the king had commanded, saying, "O people of Israel, return to the LORD, the God of Abraham, Isaac, and Israel, that he may turn again to the remnant of you who have escaped from the hand of the kings of Assyria. 7 Do not be like your fathers and your brothers, who were faithless to the LORD God of their fathers, so that he made them a desolation, as you see. 8 Do not now be stiff-necked as your fathers were, but yield yourselves to the LORD and come to his sanctuary, which he has consecrated forever, and serve the LORD your God, that his fierce anger may turn away from you. 9 For if you return to the LORD, your brothers and your children will find compassion with their captors and return to this land. For the LORD your God is gracious and merciful and will not turn away his face from you, if you return to him."

Jeremiah 3:22 (ESV) "Return, O faithless sons; I will heal your faithlessness." "Behold, we come to you, for you are the LORD our God.

Hosea 6:1 (ESV) "Come, let us return to the LORD; for he has torn us, that he may heal us; he has struck us down, and he will bind us up.

Chapter 8
THE CONSEQUENCES OF BACKSLIDING

One problem with a backslidden heart is the guilt we might carry around because of our sins. Another is the damage we do physically, mentally, emotionally, financially, and relationally while in our sins. The Father calls us back to Him and can completely restore what we lost during backsliding.

Although we will be forgiven and restored, the sins we commit while backsliding carry long-term consequences. For example, suppose I kill someone in a fit of anger. God will forgive me, but I may spend many years in prison. While in prison, I may suffer relational and financial issues. The Scriptures are clear in showing us that we reap what we sow.

> *Galatians 5:16 (ESV) But I say, walk by the Spirit, and you will not gratify the desires of the flesh.*

> *Galatians 6:7-8 (ESV) Do not be deceived: God is not mocked, for whatever one sows, that will he also reap. 8 For the one who sows to his own flesh will from the flesh reap corruption, but the one who sows to the Spirit will from the Spirit reap eternal life.*

A BACKSLIDING HEART

As another example, let's suppose a young Christian girl backslides and starts associating with bad company. We know from the Scriptures that bad company ruins good morals.

> *1 Corinthians 15:33 (ESV) Do not be deceived: "Bad company ruins good morals."*

Suppose the young girl has physical relations with an older man and becomes pregnant. Suppose the judicial system sentences the older man to jail time for his actions, which affects his life forever. The young girl's life has now been affected in some fashion for the rest of her life. The Lord can forgive both parties for their actions, but the consequences of those actions remain.

I will share a saying I learned as a young believer in the 1970s. "Sin will take you further than you wanted to go, keep you longer than you wanted to stay, and cost you more than you wanted to pay." If we do not desire to repent, we may need to cry out to the Father to turn us. Some say He will take us to the bottom of the pit so that all we can see is up. Then maybe our hearts of rebellion will soften, and we will repent and return to our Father's heart. The Father is calling and waiting for us to return home.

> *Psalms 80:3 (ESV) Restore us, O God; let your face shine, that we may be saved!*

Psalms 85:4 (ESV) Restore us again, O God of our salvation, and put away your indignation toward us!

Lamentations 5:21 (ESV) Restore us to yourself, O LORD, that we may be restored! Renew our days as of old—

We may try to conceal a backsliding heart, but the Father knows and judges.

Proverbs 28:13-14 (ESV) Whoever conceals his transgressions will not prosper, but he who confesses and forsakes them will obtain mercy. 14 Blessed is the one who fears the LORD always, but whoever hardens his heart will fall into calamity.

Chapter 9
GOD WILL PUNISHMENT THOSE WHO TEMPT OTHERS TO BACKSLIDE

We hear the saying, "Misery loves company," all the time. It is a very Biblical statement. It comes from the Book of Romans. People who love sin also love to get others involved in what they do. God will punish backsliders but will also punish their attempt to draw others into their sins. It never ceases to amaze me that those who love sin can't keep it to themselves. Notice how the wicked are driven to pressure the righteous to accept their sinful ways in everyday life. Notice the joy the wicked have over the evil ways of others.

Many years ago, in the 1970s, Debby and I were invited to a birthday party of work associates. I reluctantly accepted because I knew there would be alcoholic beverages served, and I personally do not drink. There were about thirty people at the party, and everyone in the room knew I was a Christian and refrained from the use of alcohol. However, throughout the night, different individuals would bring me soda spiked with some form of hard drink. I had to smell any soda offered to see if it had been spiked. They thought it funny in their attempts to slip me alcoholic beverages. This experience taught me a valuable lesson concerning the warnings we have in the Scriptures. I never placed myself in that situation again.

> *1 Corinthians 15:33 (ESV) Do not be deceived: "Bad company ruins good morals."*

In the last chapter, I used 1 Corinthians 15:33, showing that bad company ruins good morals. I used it from the Christian's point of view, showing that we need to keep Godly friends. However, looking from the other viewpoint, let's see what the Father says concerning those who tempt others into their sins. Proverbs 28:10 tells us there will be those who will tempt the righteous to sin.

> *Proverbs 28:10 (ESV) Whoever misleads the upright into an evil way will fall into his own pit, but the blameless will have a goodly inheritance.*

In Romans 1, the Apostle Paul gives us a list of those who have turned away from God and practice sins, including all forms of sexual immorality. Then, he states in Romans 1:32 that some strongly support those who commit these sins.

> *Romans 1:32 (ESV) Though they know God's righteous decree that those who practice such things deserve to die, they not only do them but give approval to those who practice them.*

A BACKSLIDING HEART

The Apostle Paul warns young Timothy of the coming trials of the last days from sinful and wicked people. These people are not just happy walking in their immoral behavior but go into house churches, leading others astray with their fleshly passions.

2 Timothy 3:1-6 (ESV) But understand this, that in the last days there will come times of difficulty. 2 For people will be lovers of self, lovers of money, proud, arrogant, abusive, disobedient to their parents, ungrateful, unholy, 3 heartless, unappeasable, slanderous, without self-control, brutal, not loving good, 4 treacherous, reckless, swollen with conceit, lovers of pleasure rather than lovers of God, 5 having the appearance of godliness, but denying its power. Avoid such people. 6 For among them are those who creep into households and capture weak women, burdened with sins and led astray by various passions,

The Apostle Paul warns Titus of deceitful and rebellious people who upset Christian families with false teachings.

Titus 1:10-11 (ESV) For there are many who are insubordinate, empty talkers and deceivers, especially those of the circumcision party. 11 They must be silenced, since they are upsetting whole families by teaching for shameful gain what they ought not to teach.

The religious leaders were happy with Judas' sin of betrayal.

> *Mark 14:10-11 (ESV) Then Judas Iscariot, who was one of the twelve, went to the chief priests in order to betray him to them. 11 And when they heard it, they were glad and promised to give him money. And he sought an opportunity to betray him.*

Our Lord's words in Matthew 18:6 are vital to understanding how God feels about those who take pleasure in causing others to stumble and sin. Think about a large stone tied around your neck, and then you are thrown into the deepest part of the ocean. Do you think the backslidden leading others into sin is a serious matter with God?

> *Matthew 18:6 (ESV) but whoever causes one of these little ones who believe in me to sin, it would be better for him to have a great millstone fastened around his neck and to be drowned in the depth of the sea.*

Chapter 10
HOW CAN WE HELP SOMEONE WHO IS BACKSLIDING?

We may readily recognize a Christian brother or sister who is backslidden, but perhaps there is one more question we need to consider. How do we help someone who is backsliding? The answer is in Galatians chapter 6. Not only is the Father active in calling the backslider to a place of repentance, but the believer walking in practical righteousness should also be proactive in restoring the backslider.

> *James 5:10-12 (ESV) As an example of suffering and patience, brothers, take the prophets who spoke in the name of the Lord. 11 Behold, we consider those blessed who remained steadfast. You have heard of the steadfastness of Job, and you have seen the purpose of the Lord, how the Lord is compassionate and merciful. 12 But above all, my brothers, do not swear, either by heaven or by earth or by any other oath, but let your "yes" be yes and your "no" be no, so that you may not fall under condemnation.*

If we are going to assist a backslidden brother toward restoration, there are some steps we need to be mindful of. First, we must do some personal examination and then seek to restore them gently.

> Galatians 6:1 (ESV) Brothers, if anyone is caught in any transgression, you who are spiritual should restore him in a spirit of gentleness. Keep watch on yourself, lest you too be tempted.

1. BREAKING DOWN THE STEPS IN GALATIANS 6:1

- ***Are they in sin?***

"Brothers, if anyone is caught in any transgression,"

Is the Christian brother or sister actually violating God's Word and character, or are they just breaking one of our pet peeves? We must first evaluate that what we are witnessing is a transgression against the Father and not one of our personal convictions that cannot be found in the Bible.

- ***Are you Spirit-filled?***

"you who are spiritual"

"You who are spiritual" is an interesting phrase. It means "one filled with and governed by the

A BACKSLIDING HEART

Spirit of God. We call it being "Spirit-filled" and not in the flesh. The Scriptures say a lot concerning the responsibilities of those who are Spirit-filled. Let's look at a few of God's commands from His Word.

> Romans 15:1 (ESV) We who are strong have an obligation to bear with the failings of the weak, and not to please ourselves.
>
> 1 Corinthians 2:15 (ESV) The spiritual person judges all things, but is himself to be judged by no one.
>
> 1 Corinthians 3:1 (ESV) But I, brothers, could not address you as spiritual people, but as people of the flesh, as infants in Christ.
>
> Hebrews 5:14 (ESV) But solid food is for the mature, for those who have their powers of discernment trained by constant practice to distinguish good from evil.
>
> James 5:19-20 (ESV) My brothers, if anyone among you wanders from the truth and someone brings him back, 20 let him know that whoever brings back a sinner from his wandering will save his soul from death and will cover a multitude of sins.

- **Go after them.**

"should restore him in a spirit of gentleness."

We go after those whom we witness to be backslidden with the same love and compassion that God goes after us. This approach means to speak the truth of God with love. It is essential to understand why their love for Jesus went cold. Learning why they departed from their first love will call for patience and grace. The restoration ministry is certainly not the time for criticism or condemnation. Don't forget backsliding is often connected to some event that has happened in their life. It may be as simple as neglect of spiritual disciplines or a great emotional or mental hurt or disappointment. It is the responsibility of those who are spiritual to help them through it. I have seen too many pastors and church members quickly "write off" the backslidden because restoring them was either too messy or required more time and effort than what the church wanted to invest.

- **Be sober-minded and watchful.**

"Keep watch on yourself, lest you too be tempted."

In counseling, there is a dynamic called transference and countertransference. Basically, it is a warning about developing an emotional and mental bond with the one you are counseling. Building an emotional or mental stronghold may cause the counselor to fall into the same sin as the one being advised.

Chapter 11
THERE IS HOPE FOR THE BACKSLIDER

With all the "bad news" about the sin of backsliding, there is also "good news." Our Heavenly Father is redemptive in nature. Since the backslider is a child of God, the Father woos him back to a place of righteousness using His chastening hand. We may fall deep, but our Heavenly Father can move faster than we can fall.

> *Hebrews 12:6 (ESV) For the Lord disciplines the one he loves, and chastises every son whom he receives."*

The Father's chastening hand is one piece of evidence that we are genuinely born again. The writer of Hebrews tells us that the Father does not chasten illegitimate children, which are the children of the enemy or those who are spiritually lost.

> *Hebrews 12:7-8 (ESV) It is for discipline that you have to endure. God is treating you as sons. For what son is there whom his father does not discipline? 8 If you are left without discipline, in which all have participated, then you are illegitimate children and not sons.*

Although the discipling hand of the Lord may seem severe at the time, it is meant to bring us back to the place of walking in His righteousness.

> Hebrews 12:9-11 (ESV) Besides this, we have had earthly fathers who disciplined us and we respected them. Shall we not much more be subject to the Father of spirits and live? 10 For they disciplined us for a short time as it seemed best to them, but he disciplines us for our good, that we may share his holiness. 11 For the moment all discipline seems painful rather than pleasant, but later it yields the peaceful fruit of righteousness to those who have been trained by it.

The essential statement we need to remember is that the Father is more committed to our spiritual walk than we are. He does not sleep or slumber, and His eyes are always on us. If we are backslidden, we can walk away from God if we choose, but not without God wooing us to the opportunity for repentance. The Holy Spirit will seek to draw us back as the prodigal son did. The Father's heart is broken over those who allow a backslidden heart to become cold, hardened, and calloused.

Chapter 12
Prayers of Confession in Turning Away From the Sin of Backsliding

In restoring a backsliding heart, the person in sin must be honest with their heart in confessing sins. It is a habit for believers to just throw a "confessing blanket prayer" out to the Father concerning our sins. Example: Father, forgive me of all my sins and anything I may have done that I am not aware of in Jesus' Name, I pray. Amen. This intercession is known as a blanket prayer where we try to cover all our sins in one simple, all-inclusive statement. We need to confess our sins by name for proper restoration. Notice in Isaiah 59:12-14 how the people's sins are named individually. The people acknowledged their sins and took full responsibility for them. This attitude is strikingly different from today, in which many believers have renamed sin in an attempt to soften the transgression and then seek to justify their immorality by placing the blame outside of themselves.

> *Isaiah 59:12-13 (ESV) For our transgressions are multiplied before you, and our sins testify against us; for our transgressions are with us, and we know our iniquities: 13 transgressing, and denying the LORD, and turning back from*

following our God, speaking oppression and revolt, conceiving and uttering from the heart lying words.

Israel had sinned greatly and was judged because she refused to repent and return to the Lord. The Assyrians attacked her in 732 BC and destroyed the nation and the land. Afterward, under the warnings of God's prophets, Judah had 130 years to repent from the same sins that Israel had done. The Father spoke through the prophet Jeremiah of the conditions of returning to the Lord. In 597 BC, the Babylonians attacked and destroyed Judah. Jerusalem and the Temple were laid waste. All of this judgment resulted from God's people refusing to confess and repent from their sins and return to the Lord.

Jeremiah 3:12-14 (ESV) Go, and proclaim these words toward the north, and say, "'Return, faithless Israel, declares the LORD. I will not look on you in anger, for I am merciful, declares the LORD; I will not be angry forever. 13 Only acknowledge your guilt, that you rebelled against the LORD your God and scattered your favors among foreigners under every green tree, and that you have not obeyed my voice, declares the LORD. 14 Return, O faithless children, declares the LORD; for I am your master; I will take you, one from a city and two from a family, and I will bring you to Zion.

A BACKSLIDING HEART

Of course, I would be wronging you if I did not include King David's incredible prayer of repentance in Psalms 51. First, we see that David cried out for God's mercy, which is not getting what he deserved. His sins weighed heavy on his soul, and he wanted the Father to blot or remove them.

> *Psalms 51:1 (ESV) To the choirmaster. A Psalm of David, when Nathan the prophet went to him, after he had gone in to Bathsheba. Have mercy on me, O God, according to your steadfast love; according to your abundant mercy blot out my transgressions.*

In Psalms 51:2-4 we see that David knew only God could wash his iniquity away. He was destined to live forever in his sins without being washed by the Lord. David acknowledged he had sinned against heaven and all the righteousness of God.

> *Psalms 51:2-4 (ESV) Wash me thoroughly from my iniquity, and cleanse me from my sin! 3 For I know my transgressions, and my sin is ever before me. 4 Against you, you only, have I sinned and done what is evil in your sight, so that you may be justified in your words and blameless in your judgment.*

David knew that he was not a sinner because he sinned but that he sinned because he was conceived as a sinner. He acknowledged that God desired to see truth and wisdom instead of iniquity.

> *Psalms 51:5-6 (ESV) Behold, I was brought forth in iniquity, and in sin did my mother conceive me. 6 Behold, you delight in truth in the inward being, and you teach me wisdom in the secret heart.*

David is getting to the meat of his prayer now. He knew he needed to be washed from his sins. We know our sins carry deep spiritual significance in separating us from God. However, they also have a tremendous mental, emotional, and relational load that sometimes is overwhelming. James tells us to confess our faults one to another so that we might be healed.

> *James 5:16 (ESV) Therefore, confess your sins to one another and pray for one another, that you may be healed. The prayer of a righteous person has great power as it is working.*

Notice in Psalms 51:7-10 that David cried out to be purged with hyssop. He knew his sins would be forgiven, and his heart would be made clean and pure as snow. He asked the Father to create a clean heart within him and renew his spirit.

> *Psalms 51:7-10 (ESV) Purge me with hyssop, and I shall be clean; wash me, and I shall be whiter than snow. 8 Let me hear joy and gladness; let the bones that you have broken*

A BACKSLIDING HEART

rejoice. 9 Hide your face from my sins, and blot out all my iniquities. 10 Create in me a clean heart, O God, and renew a right spirit within me.

David understood the danger of maintaining a backsliding heart. He was concerned in Psalms 51:11-13 that God would forever separate Himself from David and the presence of the Holy Spirit would be taken away. David reminded God of the rewards of his restoration from sin. He would teach others the danger of sinning and maintaining a backslidden position within the heart.

Psalms 51:11-13 (ESV) Cast me not away from your presence, and take not your Holy Spirit from me. 12 Restore to me the joy of your salvation, and uphold me with a willing spirit. 13 Then I will teach transgressors your ways, and sinners will return to you.

Chapter 13
PROMISES FROM THE FATHER THAT HE WILL PARDON THE BACKSLIDER

The Father is not like man in His promises in that He cannot lie. His Word is "Yes and Amen" for His glory. He is not slack in the promises that He has made to us. What the Father has spoken will be made good. God's Word is like money in the bank. You can withdraw it at any time.

> *Numbers 23:19-20 (ESV) God is not man, that he should lie, or a son of man, that he should change his mind. Has he said, and will he not do it? Or has he spoken, and will he not fulfill it? 20 Behold, I received a command to bless: he has blessed, and I cannot revoke it.*

> *2 Peter 3:9 (ESV) The Lord is not slow to fulfill his promise as some count slowness, but is patient toward you, not wishing that any should perish, but that all should reach repentance.*

> *Jeremiah 36:3 (ESV) It may be that the house of Judah will hear all the disaster that I intend to do to them, so that every one may turn from his evil way, and that I may forgive their iniquity and their sin."*

A BACKSLIDING HEART

Ephesians 1:7 (ESV) In him we have redemption through his blood, the forgiveness of our trespasses, according to the riches of his grace,

1 John 1:9 (ESV) If we confess our sins, he is faithful and just to forgive us our sins and to cleanse us from all unrighteousness.

Jeremiah 33:8 (ESV) I will cleanse them from all the guilt of their sin against me, and I will forgive all the guilt of their sin and rebellion against me.

If you are reading this and your love for God has grown cold, I plead with you to come home. Come back to the heart of the Father.

Chapter 14
THE FATHER WILL HEAL THE HEART OF THE BACKSLIDER

God is willing and able to forgive, redeem, and restore the backslider. Studying the Bible's doctrines of substitutionary atonement, justification, sanctification, and glorification would tell us that our Lord Jesus Christ paid a debt that He did not owe because we owed a debt we could not pay. Therefore, He paid the total debt for the sins of mankind so we could be redeemed. In our redemption, it was like Christ took our place for our judgment, and we took His place of being righteous before the Father. When we were washed with the blood of our Lord Jesus Christ, we were cleansed from all sin and seen as though we had not sinned. We were sanctified or set apart as holy before the King of Glory for His use.

> *Jeremiah 3:21-22 (ESV) A voice on the bare heights is heard, the weeping and pleading of Israel's sons because they have perverted their way; they have forgotten the LORD their God. 22 "Return, O faithless sons; I will heal your faithlessness." "Behold, we come to you, for you are the LORD our God.*

A BACKSLIDING HEART

Hosea 14:4 (ESV) I will heal their apostasy; I will love them freely, for my anger has turned from them.

2 Corinthians 5:18-21 (ESV) All this is from God, who through Christ reconciled us to himself and gave us the ministry of reconciliation; 19 that is, in Christ God was reconciling the world to himself, not counting their trespasses against them, and entrusting to us the message of reconciliation. 20 Therefore, we are ambassadors for Christ, God making his appeal through us. We implore you on behalf of Christ, be reconciled to God. 21 For our sake he made him to be sin who knew no sin, so that in him we might become the righteousness of God.

We patiently await until the day when we cast off this temporal body, which is perishing, and put on the eternal glorified body, and live forever in His presence.

Chapter 15
THERE IS A BLESSING FOR THOSE WHO KEEP THEMSELVES FROM A HEART OF BACKSLIDING

Happy is the man who has set his face like a flint and does not backslide. One of the joys is that his personal testimony is not damaged by people seeing a period of backsliding. If our Christian life is like a roller coaster, people will not take us seriously when we share Biblical truths. They will be like, "Oh no, here he goes again. But no matter, it won't last long before he is back doing his old lifestyle."

> *Isaiah 26:2-4 (ESV) Open the gates, that the righteous nation that keeps faith may enter in. 3 You keep him in perfect peace whose mind is stayed on you, because he trusts in you. 4 Trust in the LORD forever, for the LORD GOD is an everlasting rock.*

> *Colossians 1:21-23 (ESV) And you, who once were alienated and hostile in mind, doing evil deeds, 22 he has now reconciled in his body of flesh by his death, in order to present you holy and blameless and above reproach before him, 23 if indeed you continue in the faith, stable*

A BACKSLIDING HEART

and steadfast, not shifting from the hope of the gospel that you heard, which has been proclaimed in all creation under heaven, and of which I, Paul, became a minister.

Backsliding is a dangerous place to be with the Lord. Staying in a backslidden position can be deadly. However, there are great blessings ahead for those who have driven a stake in the ground and declared they will not return to their old ways but will serve the Lord, even if they must do so alone.

We may need to separate ourselves from friends and, yes, even family members to stand faithfully with the Father and His Word, but in doing so, we have been promised that we will prosper.

Psalms 1:1-3 (ESV) Blessed is the man who walks not in the counsel of the wicked, nor stands in the way of sinners, nor sits in the seat of scoffers; 2 but his delight is in the law of the LORD, and on his law he meditates day and night. 3 He is like a tree planted by streams of water that yields its fruit in its season, and its leaf does not wither. In all that he does, he prospers.

If your heart has grown cold, seek Him while He may be found. Remember, Return, and Repent. And then do the former things you did when you were a passionate lover of the King of Glory. Don't come to the place where God must remove your light.

> *Revelation 2:4-5 (ESV) But I have this against you, that you have abandoned the love you had at first. 5 Remember therefore from where you have fallen; repent, and do the works you did at first. If not, I will come to you and remove your lampstand from its place, unless you repent.*

Stand, and having done all else, continue to stand even when it is hard and unpopular. Choose to be a vessel of honor and walk in practical righteousness.

> *Ephesians 6:10-11 (ESV) Finally, be strong in the Lord and in the strength of his might. 11 Put on the whole armor of God, that you may be able to stand against the schemes of the devil.*

> *Ephesians 6:13-14 (ESV) Therefore take up the whole armor of God, that you may be able to withstand in the evil day, and having done all, to stand firm. 14 Stand therefore, having fastened on the belt of truth, and having put on the breastplate of righteousness,*

Choose to be the tree planted by the streams of the Father's living water. Your leaf will not wither, and all that you do will prosper.

> *Psalms 1:3 (ESV) He is like a tree planted by streams of water that yields its fruit in its*

season, and its leaf does not wither. In all that he does, he prospers.

The call of the Father is clear for us in Revelation 2. We are to remember, repent, and do our first works.

Revelation 2:4-5 (ESV) But I have this against you, that you have abandoned the love you had at first. 5 Remember therefore from where you have fallen; repent, and do the works you did at first. If not, I will come to you and remove your lampstand from its place, unless you repent.

CHARLES W MORRIS

MORE BOOKS BY CHARLES MORRIS

1. The Four Positions Of The Holy Spirit
2. Born Again
3. The 10 Characteristics Of A Spirit-Filled Church
4. The Covenant Of Salt
5. The Parable Of The Four Soils
6. The Five Evidences Of Salvation
7. Hosea
8. Preparing Ourselves To Hear The Voice Of God
9. Fifteen Ways To Hear The Voice Of God
10. The 24 Qualifications Of An Elder
11. The Bible Proves Itself True
12. Experiencing The Beauty Of Brokenness
13. Places Where God And Man Meet
14. Your Dash
15. Chart Your Path
16. The Five Witnesses Of Salvation
17. How Do I Write A Book?
18. Hosea Introduction
19. Hosea 1:1-3
20. Hosea 1:4-5
21. Hosea 1:6-7
22. Hosea 1:8-9
23. Hosea 1:10-11
24. A Willingness To Be Taught
25. Luke 15
26. The Chronological Book Of End Times

27. Is Atheism Dead?
28. Wherever You Go Travel Journal Adults
29. Wherever You Go Travel Journal Teens
30. The Topical Journal Veterans
31. The Topical Journal Women
32. The Topical Journal Adults
33. Wherever You Go Travel Journal Men
34. The Topical Journal Men
35. Is Religion Dead?
36. Unleashed
37. I Feel Like I'm Losing My Faith
38. We Need Faith
39. Is Christian Immaturity Dead?
40. The Parable Of The Wheat And Tares
41. Go Tell It On The Mountain
42. The Cost Of Discipleship
43. The Power Of One More
44. The Gospel According To Luke
45. The Gospel According To Jesus
46. I Am Light & Dark Blue, Light & Dark Pink, Peach, & Gold
47. Six Enemies Of Faith
48. Six Dangerous Love Affairs
49. Overcoming Fear
50. Don't Give The Enemy A Seat At Your Table
51. A Course In Miracles
52. Angels
53. The Holy Spirit: Do I Have To Speak In Tongues?
54. Host The Holy Ghost
55. Defeating The Sin Within Me

ABOUT THE AUTHOR

CHARLES is passionate about the manifested presence of God, seeing the Father's authentic Biblical leadership taking their position of grace and authority, and working towards seeing true Biblical unity in the Spirit and unity of the faith within the body of Christ. He served the Lord and others in the pastorate for more than 40 years, leading almost 8,000 people to a personal knowledge of the Lord Jesus Christ.

In 2000, Charles founded Raising the Standard International Ministry (RSIM), assisting pastors, spiritual leaders, and the body of Christ to pursue these key objectives.

In 2018, Charles founded Raising the Standard International Publishing (RSIP) to self-publish his books and assist other believers in pursuing their dream of getting the passion of their hearts printed. Charles has written and published more than 50 books.

Charles is an evangelist and church planter known for his uncompromising approach to God's Word without denominational or religious bias. He has the unique ability to use word pictures to paint the truth of God's Word. His uncompromising message instills the virtues of honor and respect for other believers, whether they are in a position of authority, being a peer, or have been entrusted to his shepherding and care. Charles' key message for believers is to die daily to self, embrace the beauty in personal brokenness, and walk in faith and the power of the Holy Spirit.

Made in United States
Orlando, FL
07 December 2023